A Guide to
CONNEMARA'S
EARLY CHRISTIAN SITES

ANTHONY PREVITÉ

PUBLISHED BY OLDCHAPEL PRESS

First published in 2008 by

Oldchapel Press
Oldchapel, Oughterard
Co. Galway, Republic of Ireland

www.oldchapelpress.net

Cover Photo: Early Cross on MacDara's Island

ISBN: 978-0-9560062-0-2

Layout and design by Connemara Publications, Clifden, Co. Galway
Printed in Ireland

CONTENTS

"Ruins are not empty.
They are sacred places full of presence."
(John O'Donohue)

Acknowledgements

Martin O'Malley, Ballyconneely, Tomás O'Gaora, Carna, Sean Cunnane, Jerry Moran and John Coyne, Inishbofin, for their local knowledge and such willing help with the various marine excursions.

Michael Gibbons, Clifden, for his encouragement and for kindly reading through this project to keep me archaeologically correct. Most especially for all his skills and knowledge which he has so generously shared with the hundreds who have accompanied him on his many walks throughout the Connemara countryside and for awakening our awareness to the archaeological riches of the past that surround us. This is not only locally but internationally.

Dave Hogan, Letterfrack, ecologist, historian, musician and language expert, who has so generously assisted with the standardising of the Irish place names and other important editorial corrections.

Don Brown, Bundowlish, for his valuable and skilful assistance with items of photography, especially of High Island. My brother, Nicholas, Burghill, for his excellent photograph of the Egyptian felucca on the Nile, and Noel Mannion for his photos of Streamstown and Bunowen.

My son, Oliver, Moycullen, who has assisted me with some of the foundation sketches of impenetrable sites.

Noel Mannion and Catherine Lavoie of Connemara Publications, Clifden, for their enthusiasm, skill, good humour, encouragement and absolute professionalism in bringing this publication to fruition.

To the late John O'Donohue of Glentrasna for his constant encouragement and with whom I have shared the sacred mysteries among the ancient ruins.

To my wife, Christina, for her patience with me and her keen eye as proof-reader and occasional companion on field visits.

The seed for my interest in these early sites was a combination of firstly being infected by the enthusiasm for this subject from the former lecturer in History and Professor of Pastoral Theology at TCD and Principal of the Church of Ireland Theological College, the late Canon Jim Hartin; and secondly having read Bob Quinn's most comprehensive and exciting researches contained in his books 'Atlantean' (1986) and the 'Atlantean Irish' (2004). Such people create a hugely valuable awareness of our historical and cultural background and present day contexts for which we should be humbly grateful.

PREFACE

The islands and coastline of Connemara are alive with the constantly changing colours, clouds, sunlight or rain, sometimes disappearing and reappearing from blankets of sea fog and squalls of rain. The winter storms then purging the landscapes before the arrival of Spring. It was with such a kaleidoscope of seasons that the monks and eremitics of these often isolated and precarious sites lived their lives on the edge of what was a maritime highway reaching from North Africa to Scandinavia. It was these who introduced the spiritual tradition into Gaelic society as founded by the desert ascetics of the 3rd and 4th centuries.

So, the purpose of this little publication is in part a response to the frequently asked questions relating to the arrival of Christianity on our shores, and also to awaken an awareness of and to introduce the reader to the valuable history and heritage signified by these many coastal sites that surround the shores of Connemara.

In cases such as High Island and MacDara's Island this heritage has been well recognised and the ancient remains either restored or preserved and much valuable archaeological work undertaken. In other cases the remains are sadly disappearing or being destroyed through neglect or careless vandalism.

This book is primarily a guide to these unique sites of the past, yet not an academic research. The reader will hopefully further their interest with considerable benefit by consulting the acknowledged experts referred to in the bibliography such as Tim Robinson, Bob Quinn, Jenny White Marshall, Grellan D Rourke etc., who have researched and contributed so widely to this subject.

Anthony Previté, Connemara, 2008

NOTE ON CONNEMARA

The name of Connemara has an interesting background. It is said that in about the 4th century, the Gaelic Kings of Connacht sent the warlike *Conmaicne*, or the *Tribe of Comac* (one of *Queen Maeve's* lovechildren) to various corners of the province in a plantation scheme to expand their power and ensure the submission of such peoples as the *Fir Bolg*. One branch of the *Conmaicne* was directed to settle by the sea and became the *'Conmaicne Mara'*, or the *Tribe of Conmac by the Sea*, and from them Connemara took its name. The name was apparently only shortened to 'Connemara' in the 18th century. In legendary history a more likely derivation of the term *Conmaicne* is that it refers to the "dog sons" with the *Conmaicne* being the dog sons of the sea.

NOTE ON DATING

Early Christian	AD ca	500 – 1200
Medieval		1170 – 1350
Late Medieval		1350 – 1600
Romanesque Style		1130 – 1200
Transitional Style		1200 – 1250
Gothic Style		1250 – 1600

Early Christian churches were rectangular with a west doorway (trabeate), a plain east window and projecting corbels or antae.

Medieval churches would have nave and chancel, i.e. enlarged oratories.

Late Medieval churches, would be simple rectangular churches with doorways on one of the sidewalls, usually the south, and the frequent traces of either a loft, an extension or a subdivision at the west end which may have been living quarters for clergy.

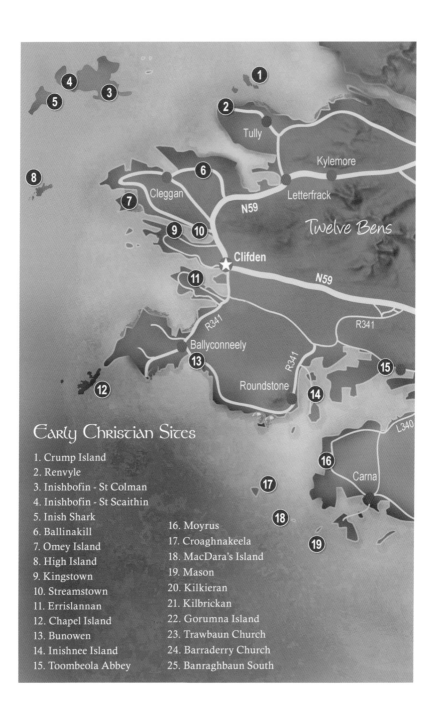

€aRly ChRisτian Siτes

1. Crump Island
2. Renvyle
3. Inishbofin - St Colman
4. Inishbofin - St Scaithin
5. Inish Shark
6. Ballinakill
7. Omey Island
8. High Island
9. Kingstown
10. Streamstown
11. Errislannan
12. Chapel Island
13. Bunowen
14. Inishnee Island
15. Toombeola Abbey

16. Moyrus
17. Croaghnakeela
18. MacDara's Island
19. Mason
20. Kilkieran
21. Kilbrickan
22. Gorumna Island
23. Trawbaun Church
24. Barraderry Church
25. Banraghbaun South

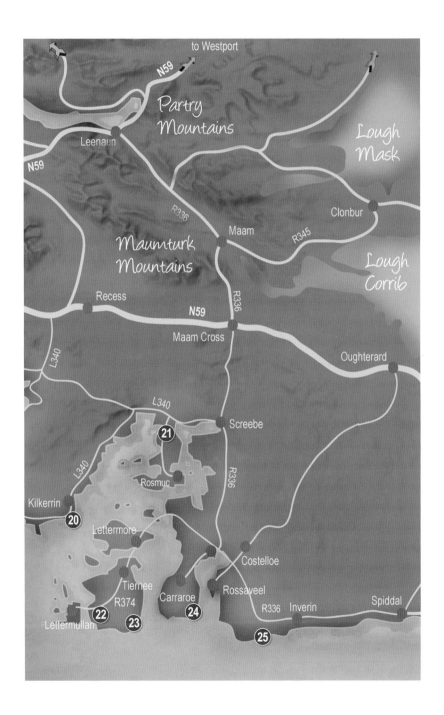

NOTE ON EARLY MARITIME HISTORY

"Following the Ice Age the first inhabitants came to Ireland, and they would obviously have come by sea. Professor Frank Mitchell in the 'Irish Landscape', puts the earliest record of men in Ireland at between 8,000 and 8,600 years ago (i.e. ca 6,000 BC), according to radio-carbon dating methods, and that they were fisherfolk as identified by their accompanying remains of fish bones found in many middens. He further suggests that this early Mesolithic culture may have come from Denmark (where similar sites have been found)."

Evidence of hunter-gatherers has also been found at Streamstown, and throughout the Corrib catchment area.

"Professor EG Bowen in 'Britain and the Western Seaways', writes, "It is abundantly clear that they must have been thoroughly familiar with sea navigation and that their skin-boats and dugouts must have been used, not only for fishing, but also for movement from one part of the coast to another.

"The ancient Gaels called their land *Eriu (Eire)* and a dozen other names besides, including *Banba*, *Fotla* and *Fáil*. In some versions of the myth, Eriu was a goddess identified with the land itself and had borne the heirs of the Sons of Mil, from whom all Milesian lineages claimed descent.

"Archaeologists identify occupation by hunter-gatherers from about 7,500 BC. Agriculture was established with the early Neolithic Age, about 4,000 BC, and in time supported a culture immortalised by a series of monumental passage tombs of which Newgrange (ca 3,000 BC) is the most celebrated. From the Bronze Age (ca 2,400 – 500 BC) there is a rich legacy of ornamental gold work and bronze instruments that are now held in trust by the Nation. The first invasion of Ireland recorded in contemporary documents was that of the Vikings, whose language provided the original of the Teutonic second element in the name 'Ire-Land'."

(Excerpt from *'Inventing the Nation - Ireland'*, RV Comerford, Professor of Modern History, NUI, Maynooth)

A NORTH AFRICAN BACKGROUND

The word 'Peregrinatio' has been ascribed as the distinct characteristic activity of some of the most important of the Celtic Saints. The interpretation of the word had been well explained in the records of a sermon c. 1000 AD commemorating the festival of St Columba:

"God counselled Abraham to leave his own country and go in pilgrimage into the land which God had shown him, to wit, the 'Land of Promise'... Now the good counsel which God enjoined here on the father of the faithful is incumbent on all the faithful; that is to leave their country and their land, their wealth and their worldly delight for the sake of the Lord of the Elements, and to go in perfect pilgrimage in imitation of Him"

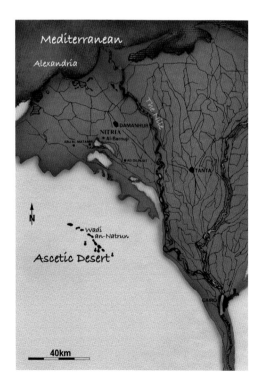

Then there was a rule known as the Rule of the Anchorites and also the Rule of Columcille, which enjoins one to 'be alone in a desert place apart in the neighbourhood of a chief monastery if you distrust in your conscience to be in the company of many'. This injunction must have been such as guided the founders of the desert hermits of Lower Egypt and Palestine, and much of Upper Egypt as well. This was however a higher degree to which only the more advanced monks might attain. This 'Third Order', as it came to be known, has been described as the general tendency to the desert, and ascribed to the end of the 6th century, claiming that in Ireland it had manifested itself much earlier.

This 'ascetic' movement epitomised by St Antony of Egypt (251-356) was a life of holiness where people did indeed withdraw from the busyness of the contemporary world to confront its suffering. Their prayers sought to help people and in particular travellers, both in the spiritual and physical sense. St Antony and his followers moved out from the Holy Lands across into North Africa where they practised this life of self-denial, and along with such as Clement of Alexandria, the Stylites and the Stoics, all of whom became generally known as the Desert Fathers. St Antony maintained that the solitary should be in a position to help others on the basis that 'he who knows himself knows God', and indeed it appears that

The Kellia Desert in Lower Egypt showing remains of monastic settlements

many came for advice and counsel. He himself had become a hermit ca 269 AD and retired to the desert ca 285 AD, when he was 34.

Research also indicates in an overwhelming manner that an active trading route by sea would already have been well-developed long before this time between this area of North Africa and the West Coast of Ireland. Along with exploratory trade, piracy and raiders, this may well have included trading in animal hides and skins used in boat coverings and any such trade by sea would in any case have been far more developed than any routes overland which would have been heavily forested. The Carthaginians are also reputed to have had principal control of the Straits of Gibraltar to protect their trade interests in Brittany.

There were also well-known tin mines in the South of England which were used by the then developed world from around the Mediterranean. In the 2nd century AD the geographer Ptolemy from Alexandria was able to name 16 tribes in Ireland, all from the coast. It is likely that he obtained this information from official records originating in Roman Britain. Some say that it may have even been safer to sail in the Atlantic waters than the Mediterranean with its ferocious storms. Many would have been well able to navigate by the stars and of course the North Star would easily lead them to the Irish waters along with the prevailing southerly and south westerly winds.

And so we come to the most remarkable of all the institutions of the ancient Celtic/Gaelic Church which is the '*Inis*', the island sanctuaries in which the more extreme of these ascetics came to live. Perhaps one of the most spectacular and best preserved, although now heavily rebuilt, of such island sanctuaries is the well-known settlement of beehive cells

Sceilig Mhichíl

near the summit of *Sceilig Mhichíl*, eight miles off the Western peninsula of County Kerry, on a sheer rock 700 ft. above the Atlantic and close to the edge of a cliff. The dedication to St Michael the Archangel, the patron Saint of high places, is not recorded until after the year 1000, so it is not known to which patron saint it was dedicated before that. There is some suggestion it may have been St Finian who was venerated on the nearby mainland. Apparently one of its monks was carried off by the Vikings in 823.

As further evidence to all this way of life we find that many other similar early Christian settlements had developed along the Western seaboard in a similar ascetic manner to the North African. Lonely stone beehive huts on isolated offshore islands and remote coasts, the beginnings of what were to become the early Irish Monastic settlements. The architectural features of these settlements are in general fairly uniform with usually one or more tiny stone beehive cells, commonly without any opening except a door, though there is sometimes also a tiny unglazed window, perhaps only for ventilation. Generally there is also a rectangular Chapel, about 12-14ft. long with a simple stone altar and one or two aumbries.

But perhaps the ascetics saw their way of life as not only one of self denial, stripping of self and of hardship in order to atone for sin to clear the pathway to God's presence, but also as the opportunity to live and be fulfilled by and in His creation. They would see God in the natural world which was another form of contemplation. As described in Hughes and Hamlin's 'Celtic Monasticism', "One looks out from his Island over the sea, listening to the waves breaking on the rocks, to the gull's cry, watching the smooth strand of clear headlands, the splendid bird-flocks, the mighty whales". The animals may have been seen as messengers of God and there are examples of the saints recording the presence at sea of dolphins, or on land the foxes, badgers, deer, etc., all of which may have attended them at their daily duties or liturgies."

Bob Quinn in his extensive research on this subject in his book 'The Atlantean', describes of Connemara, this remote spot on the edge of Europe: "From this perspective, Europe looks different. So, for that matter, does the island called Ireland. Instead of being a distant and unimportant planet on the edge of a galaxy whose axis runs East/West, Ireland can be seen as the centre of a cultural area that is oriented North and South, is based on the Atlantic seaways and stretches from Scandinavia to North Africa... The most significant and overlooked aspect of Conamara and its people is their obsession with boats and the seas. They seem to be the only large and identifiable community in Ireland which realises it inhabits an island".

He goes on to emphasise that the people of the West Coast were from birth thoroughgoing seafarers. Their roadways were on the sea rather than on land as there was virtually no traffic through what would have been a highly afforested interior. The populations were along the coast and they would have lived principally from the sea rather than from the remote mountains and bog of the hinterland. In many locations along the Connemara Coast it is common to find remains of thousands of shellfish heaped up in the constantly eroded 'middens' which give evidence of this. It is also interesting to note the similarities of the sail rigs of the Irish *pucáns*, the dipping Lug or the Lateen sail, which is the same as the *dhows* and the *feluccas* of the Nile, ancient craft still in use.

Felluca on the Nile (photo: Nicholas Previté)   *Irish Pucán*

Music also carries a huge amount of similarities to that of Arabic North Africa and the sounds of the Souk are echoed in our own traditional music. The Irish *'Sean-Nós* (or old style) singing is quite unlike any Western art and is much closer to oriental forms. The traditional Irish *Bodhrán* also has its counterpart in the *Bindir* which is the drum of Morocco. The 9th century writers in Ireland already knew of the literary wealth of the Middle East and their artistic embellishments were later copied into 12th

Dolmen   *Newgrange*

century manuscripts indicating evidence of Syrian, Spanish and Tunisian art forms. We find in the traditional Celtic lacework either an intricate maritime ropework or common snake design. In the 5th century St Brendan the Navigator is also claimed to have been to America before Leif Ericsson, and his name would be joined with the myriad of tales of wandering Irish missionaries who left these shores by sea, returning to Europe and the Mediterranean. An Irish artefact, a ringed pin similar to one from Omey, was found on the Viking settlement in Newfoundland. We can look even further back. "Down the Atlantic coasts of Europe the megaliths, or big stones, reach like gigantic stepping stones. They link places as far apart as Denmark, Scotland and southern Spain." *('Atlantean')*

These are the dolmens, menhirs and passage graves, of huge construction, which stand as a permanent testimony to the imagination and organisation of a race or races who were essentially seafarers. The passage graves of Newgrange, Knowth and Dowth in County Meath, with their massive scale, strange carvings and astronomical precision are exactly replicated by those on the coasts of Brittany and Denmark. These are similar designs, identical layouts and are located near water, indicating an undeniable relationship. There can be little doubt that the people who built these must have been in direct maritime contact over a long period of time.

"These megaliths are the most solid evidence that as far back as 3000 BC, before the pyramids of Egypt were built, people would have carried their culture up and down the Atlantic coasts. There are amazing similarities for example in the entrances to the Palace of Minos on Crete and the Newgrange passage grave in Ireland. Scholars do now agree that as far back as this time the sea was a far easier and safer form of travel when the land was forested and filled with wild animals. It would seem that the seagoing capacity of our forbears is still greatly underestimated, perhaps also because marine archaeology is still very much in its infancy. When we realise that if the waters of our planet are encroaching on land at the rate of about 1" a year, then over a span of 5000 years the remnants of centuries of coastal dwelling and remains must be well covered by water." ('Atlantean')

There would also have been a strong intellectual influence operating on our islands which must have flowed from the East Mediterranean, either directly or indirectly, as is evidenced by the remarkable skills of writing and illumination of books that are so much part of our early heritage. There can be little doubt that it was mainly through books that knowledge came to Ireland from the Eastern Church, and that it was through books as well as travel that they developed this anchorite discipline from the East.

The North African ascetics may well have lived a mortified and austere life devoted to the highest spiritual ideals which has so strongly influenced and penetrated the western world. However, alongside this was the stimulus that they also gave to intellectual life, to the spreading of reading and of book production. So this special form of sanctity practised by the early saints of the Celtic Church, poverty, asceticism, solitude, contemplation – could never have become such a widespread movement without the communion and stimulus which they derived from the early Church through the written word. It is known that these monks of the desert had carried on an active correspondence with the outside world and this communication was certainly possible through the maritime connections.

A Guide to Connemara's Early Christian Sites - Crump Island

CRUMP ISLAND

(N53°37 W009°59)

About one mile north of the shore from the Renvyle peninsula lie the three Crump Islands, *Oileán Dá Chruinne* (Island of the two Shrines), *Oileán na Naoinrí* (Calf Island), and *Oileán an Bhaile Bhig* (Island of the small settlement). Of these three the first is considerably the largest and was once occupied by a herdsman and his family.

West view of the Oratory remains

Oileán Dá Chruinne, like many other settlements off this coast, contains the remains of a simple little early Christian oratory (L6.9m x W3.95m) which is found on the south side of the island overlooking a small inlet and landing place on the rocky coast. It is perched on a small height just above the high tide line and was supposedly erected by St Ríoch, (Rue or Roc), a nephew of the Apostle of Ireland. Some history relates that this saint may at one time have been abbot of Innisbofin, an island of Lough Derg, and that a small cemetery (Salruck) on the adjoining shore at Little Killary harbour may contain his relics.

Many of the fallen stones at the east gable together with some cross marked headstones

The inside of the east window showing an aumbry to the left of the window

There is also a small cemetery which lies immediately at the east end of the church which contains several very ancient headstones. Tradition has it that these graves contain the remains of forty strangers, companions of the saint, who had accompanied him from beyond the sea. This has been preserved in oral tradition since these persons were also invoked in the Litany of St Aenghus, in the 8th century. *(From Stone's 'Life of Petrie')*

Little remains of the higher structure of this little Church but the base outline is still clearly discernable with just the east window opposite the blocked entrance doorway at the west end. There would have been no other window or opening. A boundary wall has been built up against the west gable and many of the original stones appear to be still scattered around the original building. No doubt this site would have suffered from the 9th century Viking raiders as well as the prevailing storms from the west and south west, and indeed many stones appear to have been thrown up from the rocky shore and become mixed with the original building stones. Such graves as would be normally found at such early monastic churches are usually situated outside the east gable and careful excavation would undoubtedly reveal some of these as there are several indications of headstones.

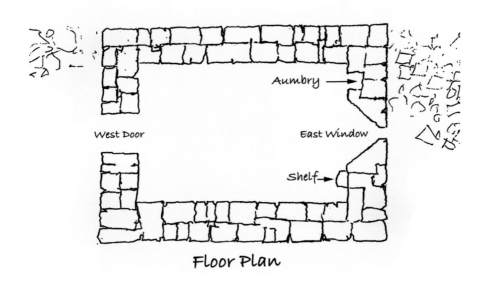

Floor Plan

RENVYLE

(N53°36 W010°02)

A mysterious group of Seven Sisters, sometimes said to be the daughters of a Leinster King or of an Omey Island chief, were known to have preached along the Connemara coast, leaving their name on a cursing stone and various holy wells at Renvyle, Cleggan Head, Aillebrack, Doon Hill and Mweenish Island. They may have finally settled on Mason Island, east of Mace harbour. This ruined medieval church here at Renvyle Point is dedicated to the Seven Daughters (L13.1m x W5m).

Church of the Seven Daughters

This old Church *(Teampaill na Seacht nInion)* is located in the old part of the Renvyle Cemetery, and was apparently built in thanks by a King for the cures his seven daughters may have received from the waters of the nearby well. Three walls survive almost intact, but most of the west wall has collapsed. The doorway, with pointed arch, is in the north wall. There is a fine single-light window with triangular head in the east wall with an altar below it and two aumbries in the south east corner. A partially

robbed window is visible in the south wall, and a later dividing wall towards the west end. Beam-slots in the south wall indicate a former loft or gallery at the west end. Possible traces of an earlier doorway are visible in the masonry of the collapsed west wall.

400m to the north east is also to be found the impressive ruins of one of the 15th/16th century O'Flaherty Castles which dominates the local landscape. It was at one time reputed to have been the home of Grace O'Malley, the famous sea queen Granuaile *(Gráinne Uí Mháille)*, around 1546 after she married Donal O'Flaherty.

opposite left: East gable, window and altar   above: South door   below: O'Flaherty castle ruins

INISHBOFIN ISLAND

(N53°36 W010°11)

From Lindisfarne Island, off the East Coast of England, came St Colman and his sixty-odd fellow monks in 667, who settled on Inishbofin *(Inis Bó Finne)* Island, some 6.5 kilometers north of High Island. Born in Connaught in 605, he was a disciple of Columba and became a monk of

Remains of medieval church

Iona, and later (661) he was to succeed St Finian as bishop of Lindisfarne in Northumbria. His episcopate of only three years was short-lived due to the controversies at the time between the Celtic and Roman Church concerning the dating of Easter, the cutting of hair (tonsure) and the local or Roman rules covering liturgy and worship. At a Synod of Whitby in England in 664 he failed to have the Celtic practices retained in the

Bullaun

face of the Romanizing party in the royal court, which resulted in King Oswy making an imperial decision that everyone was to fall in line with Rome. This resulted in St Colman removing himself and his considerable number of monks back to Iona for three years before finally coming to found his monastic community on Inishbofin Island in 668. The early Christian chapel and *clocháns* of his time are now gone, no doubt through the ensuing centuries of turmoil, and now the ruins of a medieval church, built by the O'Malleys, and the island cemetery cover that sheltered and sunny site which lies between the main harbour and the East Beach.

St Colman died on Inishbofin on February 18th, 675. His initial foundation on the island was a success, but after a short while the monastic community was torn apart by a conflict. It seems that the Irish monks were accused of leaving the monastery to go on preaching journeys during the summer at the very time when they were needed for agricultural labour. On their return in the winter, they then expected an equal share of the food with the English monks who had done all the work of bringing in the harvest. The situation caused so much discord that Colman eventually settled the English monks on the mainland, and named it Mayo of the Saxons. It became widely known as a significant centre of sanctity and learning and eventually became an Episcopal See and was mentioned in the Synod of Kells (1152). It was one of the best preserved monastic enclosures in the country.

Remains of medieval church

East gable, window and altar

This medieval church (L17.7m x 5m) has a beautiful large round-headed window in the east gable facing the Connemara mountains. There is a shallow arched doorway in the south wall which is lit by four windows in the north and south walls, two of which have now been robbed. Corbels at the west end indicate the former presence of a loft. The present west gable, containing a ruined doorway, is a later insertion, shortening the church by one third. The curving scarp line to the south-east of the church may indicate the line of a possible earlier ecclesiastical enclosure. The rectangular graveyard also contains two holy wells, two cross slabs and a bullaun, and are possibly the earliest surviving features on the site.

This is a delightful island with a population of about 140 people and is a very popular destination for holidaymakers with its many guest houses and three hotels. It is well served by regular ferries from Cleggan harbour on the mainland and has one of the safest and most accessible harbours off the west coast which is regularly used by visiting yachtsmen. On entering the outer harbour the visitor will certainly be impressed by the ancient ruins of Cromwell's 17th century Fort which dominates the harbour entrance. Legend has it that this star shaped fortification was built on the remains of a former structure attributed to a Turkish or Spanish pirate named Bosco! But the remains of this structure, as is the case with so many of these early buildings, are a testimony to those exceptional construction skills of bygone times.

opposite: Cross slabs   above: Aumbry   below: Cromwell's Fort

Children's Graveyard/early ecclesiastical enclosure

(N53°36 W010°13)

Just to the north of the village of West Quarter *(an Cheathrú Iartharach)* on Inish Bofin Island and on the east side of a hill overlooking *Loch Bó Finne*, can be found what is locally known as the Children's Graveyard, where stillborn and unbaptised children would have been buried. Such burial sites were often placed at 'boundaries' or 'frontiers' of townlands and it is interesting to see how the newer field walls have been carefully built around this site. It is also reputed to have been the early Christian site of *St Scaithin's* oratory.

There are a large number of small stones marking all the burials but little remains of any oratory other than a square formation of stones at the east end of the site which may have been a *leacht* or the possible remains of the earlier oratory. This roughly square raised area measures ca 5m x 5m and is ca 1m high. There is also a holy well, now dried up, situated some 150m to the south west.

Little seems to be known of *St Scaithin* but his name could also be written as *Scoithín* which means bloom or blossom. If this is the correct spelling then the 2nd January is ascribed as his feast day. According to Dave Hogan and Michael Gibbons in their 'Guide to the Natural History & Archaeology' of Inishbofin, *St Scáithin* may have had links with Co Kilkenny where it is reputed that his seven sons all became bishops.

Probable remains of leacht or oratory

INISH SHARK

(N53°36 W010°16)

Adjacent to Inishbofin is the island of Inish Shark *(Inis Airc)* whose last ca 23 inhabitants were evacuated from the island in 1960. It is not easy except in relatively fine weather to land at the primitive harbour/port of the island. This was partly the reason for the evacuation, since the State

Church of St Leo

gave no assistance towards its improvement. These were a people who lived in such close relationship with the sea that State help to improve facilities for their boats was essential to their survival. It was a tragedy in the island's history and as Fr Jerome Kiely wrote of it in his book, *'Seven Year Island', (1969)* "The men in Dublin were to blame..... *J'accuse!"*

above and opposite: Remains of St Leo's oratory

The remains of a 19th century Church at the south east end of the island are named after the Patron Saint of the island, St Leo.

According to the OS map (1898) the present late 19th century ruined church stands on the site of St Leo's 7th C monastery. Part of an older church has been incorporated at the north east corner where the masonry of roughly dressed blocks is much larger than elsewhere. In 1869 "the east wall with a lancet window and parts of the north and south walls" of this older church were standing. No other monuments remain. St Leo's Feast Day is observed on November 10th (previously April 11th).

From notes by James Hardiman from 'Iar-Connacht': *Roderic O'Flaherty, 1684*: "On the island are the ruins of an ancient church called *Teampaill Leo*, and near it a stone cross, *Leac Leo*. On the south shore there is a cave called *Uaimh Leo*, where the saint is said to have passed much of his time in prayer and meditation; and in it is a well dedicated to him. There is also shown a ruin called *Clochán Leo*, in which he is said to have dwelt".

The remains illustrated are of St Leo's early Christian sub-rectangular oratory. It is built on a raised area within a substantial oval shaped enclosure (17.8m x 13.5m) with a narrow entrance to the NNE. There remain some traces of a possible rectangular structure at the east end.

The only 5th century rectangular enclosures are to the east of the harbour, possibly containing early cemeteries. The reference to Leo is possibly connected to St Leo the Great who, yet as a deacon, was elected to the papacy during the years 440 to 461. He was born in 400 in Tuscany, Italy. A second Leo was elected to the papacy in 683 and was born in Sicily. In all there have been 13 Popes named Leo. The only connection found with Ireland was when in 445 Pope St Leo granted his approval to St Patrick to establish his archiepiscopal See in Armagh.

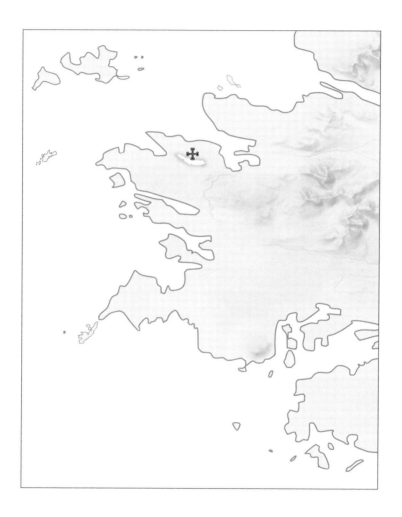

BALLINAKILL

(N53°33 W010°02)

The ruins of an ancient church lie at the foot of the hill of Cartron *(An Cartrún)* at Ballinakill *(Baile na Cille),* about three km north of the village of Cleggan, alongside the main road and overlooking Ballinakill Lough to the south. It is a poorly preserved medieval church (L20.2m x W6.1m) set within traces of a rectangular enclosure dedicated to St Ceannannach whose Well, enclosed by a circular wall, is situated about a furlong east of

West gable showing interior of window

the church. There is a doorway in the south wall. The east gable is of the 15th century church; but there is a more modern chapel at the west end, built, according to tradition, by Edward *Láidir,* or the strong, O'Flaherty, who is interred in it. A.D. 1709, appears inscribed on this chapel. This west gable has a beautiful twin light round-headed window with a small circular ope above. The interior is divided by the later wall, and a cross slab, reused as a grave marker, stands ca 12 m to the north east.

West gable showing exterior of window

St Kennanach *(Ceannanach)* is also known in the parish by the name of 'Gregory' which is said to have been his original name. There is also in the middle of the island of Inishmore (Aran Islands) a church dedicated to him which is considered to be one of the most ancient and perfect of all the ecclesiastical remains in those islands. From him it is supposed that Gregory's Sound, the passage between that island and Inishmaan, has been called. The tradition still preserved in the parish of Ballinakill is, that St Ceannanach was one of the earliest preachers of Christianity in those western parts; and that he was taken, by order of a pagan tyrant who ruled here, and beheaded near the eastern extremity of the present village of Cleggan. A heap of stones is still pointed out, one stained with the blood of his beheading, as a monument said to have been erected on the spot where he suffered.

Nearby cross slab (photo: Noel Mannion)

OCDEY ISLANÒ

(N53°32 W010°09)

From Sligo and said to be descended from Con the Hundred Fighter, came St Féichín (Little Raven), said to be a slight, black-haired youth, with his followers to the flat, sandy island of Omey *(Iomaidh)*, where he founded the Christian settlement on the northern side of the island in the 7th century. Later, a medieval church (L13.65m x W7.15m) was built there. Totally covered in sand until an illegal excavation uncovered it in

Teampaill Féichín on Omey Island

1981 as a most distinctive ruin, it is situated nearby to an earlier Bronze Age settlement which has been the subject of an archaeological survey by University College, Dublin. There is a doorway in the north wall and a lancet window set off-centre in the east gable. The west gable contains a blocked trabeate doorway also set off-centre. The church lies within a rectangular, stone-built enclosure visible to the west and south. Excavations by Tadgh O'Keefe of UCD discovered the remains of an earlier monastic enclosure on the shore to the north-west of the present church which had been largerly destroyed by wind and wave erosion. Two early crosses were also discovered on the shore here by visitors to the island.

Omey is the name from which the local parish takes its name and is an island connected to the mainland by a wide sandy strand over which one can walk at low tide. The island can be walked in about three hours and there is also St Féichín's Well to be found just above a rocky inlet to the west. It has a long dry-stone walled entrance from the sea to the well and the extra-high tide at the full moon sometimes rises up into the well through the entrance.

Following his ordination in 610, St Féichín was noted for having founded several monasteries including the well-known ones at Fore in Westmeath

Teampaill Féichín

View of Teampaill Féichín east window

(630) and Cong in Co Mayo. *The Annals of Ulster* record that he died on Omey of the Yellow Plague in 664. His Feast Day is celebrated on January 14th.

Further north west is to be found a disused graveyard *(An Cartúr Beag)* which is indicated as *Cnocán na mBan*. It is situated on the summit of a small grassy hill overlooking the north shore of the island. It was, according to local tradition, a burial place reserved for women and the burial place of Féichín's mother. It is a rough circular enclosure defined by a much degraded earthen bank which is best preserved at the south where traces of an external stone revetment can be seen. Wakeman recorded a fine early cross here now lost.

ђІGҺ ISLANÒ

(N53°32 W010°15)

High Island *(Árd Oileán)*, some 5km north west of Omey is of a totally different setting. It is inaccessible except in relatively calm weather and St Féichín, or a group of his followers were to found another monastic settlement here in 634. On this high island with its daunting cliffs these early monks had chosen a unique site on the south western side which was probably well protected by the updraught from the cliffs and a knoll

Partially restored chapel (photo: Don Brown)

between them and the settlement that shielded them from the prevailing weather. This settlement was obviously untouched for centuries and had partially crumbled over that time but there was still an amazing amount to discover here with the remains of the chapel, dwelling cells, water mill, enclosure walls, 8 graves, numerous stone crosses, as well as a reservoir and pond. This early Christian chapel (L4m x W3.2m) has a trabeate door in the west gable with a cross slab re-used as a lintel. The upper part of the gable was a later rebuilding. Traces of a window survived in a partially collapsed east gable with an altar below. A rectangular stone setting in the south west corner incorporated a small stone font. This settlement became the subject of a most comprehensive archaeological survey starting in 1980

View to mainland from island

and culminating in the publication of a highly scholarly and intriguing history written by Jenny White Marshall and Grellan D Rourke, *"High Island. An Irish Monastery in the Atlantic".(2000)* This valuable book is well worth reading as it gives a realistic and fascinating insight into the lives and capabilities of these ancient monks as well as the inevitable references to their north African and Middle Eastern influences. Following the archaeological survey there has been some careful, comprehensive and encouraging restoration of parts of this valuable site.

St Gormgal

St Gormgal was a saint also much connected with this monastic settlement and is said to have died there in either 1017 or 1018. He is reputed to have been a man of exceptional sanctity who lived as an anchorite and whose strict life had made the island famous. His Feast Day is commemorated on August 5th. It is also related that in 1014, Brian Boru, the High King of Ireland, came to High Island to make his confession to St Gormgal and a well on the island is named after the King. It seems according to the

East gable and window

Chapel and cell

Graves at east gable of the chapel (photos: Don Brown)

research of White Marshall & Rourke, that there was a Bronze/Iron Age community on this island from some time after 1000 BC. The later monastery ceased to exist but the island remained a pilgrimage destination.

above: Monastic settlement   below: Restored cell (photos: Don Brown)

A Selection of the early crosses from the island (photos: Don Brown)

kINGSTOUN

(53°30 W010°05)

Situated on the edge of the five mile inlet which is Streamstown Bay stand the very few remains of the 17th century Kill Church at Kingstown. Kingstown is that half-peninsula connected by a narrow causeway from the north side of the Sky Road circuit which goes out to the west of Clifden town.

Remains of Kill Church with ruins of Dún Castle on opposite shore

This medieval church may have been built by the O'Flaherties who were the local lords at the time and it is interesting to see from the picture that the ruins of a former O'Flaherty Castle at Doon stand directly on the opposite shore of the Bay. The church stands in a now extensive graveyard but may in earlier times have been surrounded by a slightly smaller enclosure. It is nevertheless surrounded by a vast number of stones marking hundreds of un-known burials. This is a very poorly preserved church (L13.3m x W5.10m) and only short lengths of the north and south walls survive above the foundation course, while the east gable is totally gone. There are no visible or remaining architectural details. The presence of the place name Kill, its maritime setting together with a fine early cross strongly suggests that this was an early Christian site.

Early cross slab at Kill Church, similar to one from Caher Island

above and below: The graveyard contains a number of interesting cross slabs.

STREAMSTOWN

(N53°30 W10°03)

Close to the north shore on the inner reaches of Streamstown *(Barr an tSrutha)* Bay, but densely obscured by thorn bushes, are the ruins of a medieval church, correctly known as *Teampaill Athadeirg.* Only the foundations survive and no architectural features are visible. It is located within a modern oval graveyard.

West view

What can be seen of the remaining foundations (L 13m x W 6m) suggest that here was the normal rectangular church of the age with an extension to the west which may have been living quarters.

above: North view   below: Obscured site of Teampaill Athadeirg (photos: Noel Mannion)

In these heavily overgrown remains, little can be discerned of the original stonework but parts of the north wall and east gable can just be seen on the left of this picture. Below is a sketch of the probable church foundations as determined by such scattered stone remains as could be reached.

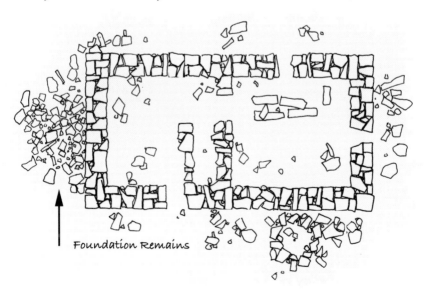

Foundation Remains

CRRISLANNAN

(N53°28 W010°03)

On the north shore of *Loch na Cille* on the Errislannan *(Iorras Fhlannáin)* peninsula are Kilflannan *(Cill Fhlannáin)*, a ruined medieval church, Tobar Flannan *(Tobar Fhlannáin)*, the holy well, and St Flannan's Bed. They are all dedicated to St Flannan of Killaloe. Kilflannan is a small very poorly preserved and overgrown medieval church (L10.3m x W4.5m). The only

Ruins of medieval church of St Flannan, Errislannan

surviving features are a plain doorway in the west wall and the Morris family tomb in the interior. The oldest part of the graveyard, oval in plan, surrounds the church. To the south of the church is a *leacht* consisting of a dry stone wall, with a niche, set into the natural slope.

above: Niche in wall of St Flannan's leacht
below: St Flannan's Stone presently kept at Errislannan Manor. The church at one time contained quite an elaborate medieval tomb, containing remains of the lordly patron. A surviving fragment depicts a portion of an angel, similar to that found in east Galway abbeys (Clonfert).

St Flannan was the son of a 7th century Irish chieftan, Turlough, King of Thomond. He entered Molua's monastery at Killaloe and may have become an abbot there. In any event he made a pilgrimage to Rome where Pope John IV consecrated him in Episcopal orders in 640. On his return he then became bishop of Killaloe. He was apparently a great preacher and travelled extensively within Ireland. His Feast Day is observed on December 18th.

To the left and within the chapel walls is the Morris family tomb with the following inscription:

"Orate pro animaeus
Familae Morris
Quorum corpora
In hac ecclesia
sepeliuntur"

Morris family tomb

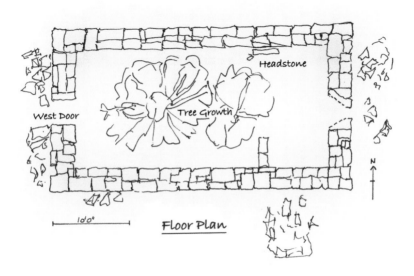

Headstone

West Door

Tree Growth

N

10'0"

Floor Plan

CHApEL ISLANò

(N53°23 W010°12)

Situated on the east side of Chapel Island *(Oileán an Teampaill)* close to the remote and windswept Slyne Head Lighthouse, is found the ancient Chapel dedicated to St Cáillín. Close to the shore of this little island stands this beautifully situated and preserved early Christian church (L7.2m x W4.75m). It is perhaps reached only by private arrangement with a local fisherman but well worth a visit. There is also a small 'bothy' on the

St Cáillíns Chapel

island where fishermen would sometimes stay during particular fishing seasons, and nearby is always a large colony of seals which are ever curious observers of any visitor. This little church is a lovely example of the early monastic structures and was cleverly situated under the shoulder of a massive outcrop of rock which has obviously sheltered it over the centuries from the prevailing weather on this wild and bleak spot.

Until fairly recently there were some graves of the monks or abbots situated outside the east gable of the Church, but the outlines, borders and other remains of these have now been washed away by the ever increasing and often very stormy and violent high tides. Nevertheless it is impressive to see how well this structure has survived and it is interesting to surmise as to what type of roofing would have been used at that time. It was obviously not stone which dates it later than the chapel on MacDara's Island, but it could have been wooden shingles since there would have been much forestry on the mainland, or more likely have been thatched with straw or the local 'sedge' grass. Two projecting corbels survive at the east and west ends of the north side-wall. There is a trabeate doorway in the west gable and a flat-headed window in the east gable together with an altar and aumbry.

Closer to the mainland and on the peninsula reaching out to Slyne Head is St Cáillín's Well, *Tobar Cháillín*, in the townland of Keeraunmore, which is reputed to have had great curative powers. It is confidently

St Cáillíns Well

View of the chapel from sea level

View of east gable from west door

East window and aumbry

believed that holy wells can never run dry, although the contrary has been frequently witnessed.

St Caillín was a bishop, a disciple of St Benign, and who is worshipped in his abbey of Fenagh *(Fidhnac)* in County Leitrim. He was also kinsman of the *Conmaicne* and had studied in Rome. He was the son of *Niata,* descended from *Rudhraighe,* whose grandson, *Fergus Mac Roigh,* flourished at the beginning of the Christian Era. His mother, *Deighe,* was the granddaughter of *Dubhthac,* the chief poet of King *Laoghaire* in the time of St Patrick. His Feast Day is celebrated on November 13th and remains a popular pilgrimage with people from Errismore and other parts of Connemara.

BUNOUEN

(N53°24 W010°06)

St Flannan was also the Patron Saint of the parish of Ballindoon *(Baile an Dúin)*, the townland of the dun or fort, and the remains of the parish church, also dedicated to St Flannan were once to be found near the shore at the foot of *Cnoc a' Dúin* hill. The present church was apparently the chapel of the Geoghegan family. There is a plain doorway in the west gable and a possible blocked doorway in the south wall as well as

Chapel of St Flannan at Bunowen

a flat-headed window in the east wall and two others in the north and south walls. A graveslab lies within the building and a small unenclosed graveyard lies immediately to the north east. In 1838 only a fragment of the south wall of the earlier church at the east end of *Cnoc a' Dúin* survived and none of it is now extant.

The little church of St Flannan can be seen on the right of the picture

Pictured above is the ruined Castle built by Richard Geoghegan at Bunowen *(Bun Abhainn Mhór)* in 1838. He was the descendant of a Cromwellian transplantee from County Westmeath. The stones used were from the ruins of a former O'Flaherty Castle nearby to the east and the medieval church. The castle later passed to John Augustus O'Neill, then to the Blake family and finally to the Congested Districts Board in 1909, after which it was de-roofed and fell into disrepair.

above: Chapel of St Flannan opposite: Burial ground showing Geoghegan tomb (photos: N Mannion)

INISHNEE ISLAND

(N53°23 W009°53)

On Inishnee Island *(Inis Ní)*, 2 miles south south east of the bridge linking the island to the main road, can be found the few remains of an ancient Chapel and Well, dedicated to St Mathias (L10m x W3.7m). This little medieval chapel is situated on the middle section of the island

St Mathias Chapel

and on a commanding site overlooking a part of Bertraghboy Bay. Sadly the only part of the chapel still standing is the south wall with its flat-headed doorway and an aumbry set into the wall. Apparently some stones may have been removed over time for use elsewhere, although a good few remain among the rubble which are now well covered by grass and other growth.

A rectangular graveyard now surrounds the chapel, but there may well have been a smaller circular one in former times. What may have been the original enclosure contains a large number of ancient and unmarked burials. Just to the north east of the chapel are the remains of what seems to be an ancient altar *(leacht)* or burial, on which is mounted an upright limestone pillar-stone accented with a linear carved cross which was common to the islands and coastal sites of the west throughout the early Christian period.

above: Remaining south wall and door below: Cemetery sign opposite: Cross slab

Reilig
naom maitiú
———
Cemetery

A Guide to Connemara's Early Christian Sites - Toombeola

⊂oomβeol∧

(N53°25 W009°51)
Just south of the Toombeola Bridge on the estuary of the Ballynahinch River and on a raised area within the graveyard is the probable site of a Friary established in 1427 by the Dominicans of Athenry. This was a sister house of the Carmelite or White friary which had also been built at Ballynahinch in 1356, of which nothing remains. This is reputed to have been destroyed in the 16th century, and its stones used to build the castle at Ballynahinch.

Toombeola church (Tuaim Beola)

The ruins of the present 19th century church consist of a rectangular building (L8.2m x W4.8m) with a curved doorway in the west wall, narrow flat-headed windows at either end of the east wall and a recess in the south wall. The site of a holy well is reputed to lie just outside the oval graveyard to the west south west. The graveyard is heavily overgrown in the summer months which makes access to the abbey very difficult. It is said that the monks of Toombeola were ultimately attacked and turned out of their church by Cromwell's soldiers.

above: Main entrance   opposite top: East gable niche   opposite bottom: North window

CDOYRUS

(N53°20 W009°52)

On the nearby mainland just about a mile from Mace harbour and near the shore are the ruins of the medieval parish church (L13.42m x W7.3m) of Moyrus *(Maoras)* which is also dedicated to St MacDara. It is one of few relatively well preserved churches in the area. Surrounded by a modern graveyard it occupies a very picturesque setting on the edge of the sea.

Remains of Moyrus Parish Church

The south doorway has a chamfered round-headed arch and hood-moulding with decorated terminals on its inner face. The outer face has been robbed since the early 19th century. There is a lancet window in the east gable, a small chamfered window in the South wall and traces of a second doorway in the north wall. As with nearly all these churches the fine stonework was done with limestone imported from Aran.

above and opposite: East gable window and south door, both remaining intact from the inside

CROAGHNAKEELA ISLAND

(N53°19 W009°58)

Two miles north west of St MacDara's Island is Croaghnakeela Island *(Cruach na Caoile)* of 142 acres, also called Deer Island since it was once stocked with deer. Now uninhabited and mostly covered in heather it is a difficult island to land on except in calm weather. There is a small automated lighthouse located near the southern point which is also the most suitable place for landing.

Light beacon at south east shore

Whilst only the remains of a small rectangular Chapel and Well are recorded on the island, a recent visit has revealed what seems to have been a considerable, but as yet undocumented, settlement probably dating to the early Christian period.

above: Outline of probable church, leacht and enclosure wall with other remains on top left and right. opposite page, top left: Stone from the collapsed leacht at west end of church top right: St Keelan's well middle left: Dolmen style structure middle right and bottom: Possible remains of an early oratory and south door. East view shows south door on the left. Note that these remains are closer to the shore than the other four that were found.

Some have said that it was originally dedicated to St Brendan, one of the principal saints of Ireland and well-known navigator. It is certain that he would have travelled in these parts and there is also a graveyard dedicated to him, Ollabrendan, on Omey Island, together with a holy well and monument on Inishnee Island across the bay from Roundstone village. However, it is more widely accepted that St Keelan (*St Caolánn*), meaning 'slender lad', may have been associated with this island which would reflect the actual background to its name. He was also a monk of the 7th century and apparently wrote a 'Life of St Brigid' in latin verse. St Caolánn may well have built the first little chapel on this island but he was also a monk of the abbey on Inisketair, an island in Lough Derg in the River Shannon.

It is interesting to note that Croaghnakeela Island is the most northerly of a trio of islands in this particular area with monastic remains, i.e., St MacDara's Island and Mason Island, both to the south but all within two miles of each other. There might well have been a close relationship between the settlers of all three.

The three other structures found on this island were less easily identifiable. One to the north and near to the former herd's cottage, one under the scarp and another to the south near the light beacon.

opposite left: Northern site   above: Southern remains with MacDara's Island in the background below: Site close under the escarpment

CDACÒARA'S ISLANÒ

(N53°18 W009°55)

Connemara's early Christian heritage is well attested to by the presence of the many monastic settlements found on our coastline and off-shore islands, together with the well-known saints associated with them.

St MacDara's Chapel with a Bád Mór in background

One of the most well known of these is St MacDara who reputedly came from Aran and is recorded as having been of a strong and argumentative character. This may have been the principal power with which he held his band of followers together as they established their monastic settlement in the 6th century on the island, which bears his name. This relatively barren island of some 60 acres to the south of Roundstone village and west of Ard Bay is usually accessible on boats from Roundstone Harbour or Mace Harbour which lies to the east.

This early Christian chapel, possibly replacing an earlier wooden structure, is quite definitely one of the most striking antiquities in the area and also featured in a series of definitive Irish architectural stamps in the 1980's. The present building has been heavily restored, robbing it of some of its authenticity. McDara's abbey prospered so well that in the 8th/9th centuries the monks were reputed to be copying the mainland style of high crosses by creating cross-slabs with stone brought over from Aran, making deeply carved interlace patterns.

Round-headed window in west wall

Restored roof and finial reproduction

This settlement situated on the east shore of the island close to a natural landing place consists of the well-preserved chapel (L4.47m x W3.43m) with evidence of three collapsed former beehive cells and enclosure wall nearby.

There is a trabeate doorway in the west wall, a round-headed window in the east wall and a flat-headed one in the south wall. Projecting antae on the east and west walls continue up the gable to the apex of the roof which is composed of stone flags. The decorated finial is a reproduction of the original found in 1884 and subsequently lost during its restoration. The replica was placed in its prominent position along with the restoration of the partially collapsed roof by the Office of Public Works in the mid 1970's. Beside the east gable is a rectangular area (1.8m x 0.82m) defined by boulders and a slab, said to be the saint's 'bed'.

Little seems to be known of the background of St MacDara himself but there is a very fine article on the island's archeological heritage written by JF Bigger, MRIA, which was published in 1896 in the Journal of the

1943 MacDara's Day Pattern (photo: © Fáilte Ireland Photographic Library)

Royal Society of Antiquaries of Ireland, and reproduced in the Journal of the Connemara Heritage Group in 1995.

The Saint's festival is celebrated on the 16th July each year when Mass is held at the east gable end of the chapel *(Teampall Mhic Dara)* for those travelling out for the day from the mainland in an amazing flotilla of boats. There is also a local tradition that boats dip their sails when passing in reverence to the Saint who is considered one of the Patron Saints to the local sailors.

opposite page: Pattern day pilgrims arriving by sea top left and below: MacDara's Day Pattern
top right: 1943 MacDara's Day Pattern (photo: © Fáilte Ireland Photographic Library)

MASON ISLAND

(N53°18 W009°53)

Eight kilometres south east of the entrance to Bertraghboy Bay lies Mason Island *(Oileán Máisean)*, an attractive, semi inhabited island of 100 acres with many ruins depicting an exceptional art in stone masonry as well as many very well built stonewalls around the fields and boreens. Sadly there are many cattle roaming freely around the island which are causing much damage to this stonework. Access is via a well built stone-built harbour (1898) at the north west of the island which replaced a previous shelter *(An tAircín)*. There were apparently some twenty one families living on the island before it was finally evacuated in 1952.

Sub-rectangular graveyard with portal stones

Remains of early Christian oratory

In a slight hollow near the centre of this island is a poorly preserved early Christian oratory (L7.8m x W4.9m) with a trabeate doorway placed off-centre in the north wall, and a robbed window in the south wall.

Immediately to the north is a small sub-rectangular graveyard (17.8m x 16.2m) defined by a slab-revetted stone wall. Its original entrance at the west end is flanked by tall stones. The interior contains a rectangular *Leacht*, much collapsed with two cross slabs and a bullaun.

Another ruined *Leacht* lies ca 8m west of the graveyard which because of its circular and seemingly revetted stones could easily be confused with a collapsed *clochán*. Another pair of enigmatic portal stones stand 12m east of the church at the entrance to this ecclesiastical enclosure which could indicate that it was an important and well-developed settlement. It is also said that the Seven Daughters may have finally settled here having travelled extensively throughout Connemara *(see Renvyle)*.

top left: Portal stones   middle left: Bullaun   top right: Cross slab   below: Leacht

KILKIERAN

(N53°19 W009°44)

Six miles east of Carna in the harbour village of Kilkieran *(Cill Chiaráin)* and standing on the east facing slope of *An Bhinn Bhuí* are the scant remains of a little chapel or oratory dedicated to St Ciarán of Clonmacnoise. These remains consist of a small, poorly preserved, early Christian oratory (L3.8m x W2.8m) with only the foundation and one or two courses of stonework visible. No architectural features survive. There is also a holy well nearby at which the saint's day is celebrated on September 9th.

Remains of St Kieran's oratory

St Kieran

St Ciarán, we are grateful and give thanks
for your Well and water of life, full of strength and goodness.
Thanks for cured people both young and old
that finally they are ready for Heaven.

This saint found no path that was laid
but that laid directly to the King of Heaven.
And St Enda stood by him
And ordinary people who welcomed him in

St Kieran was born in Roscommon, Connacht, the son of Beoit, a carpenter. He studied at St Finian's school at Clonard and taught the daughters (The Seven Daughters?) of the King of Cuala, as he was considered the most learned monk at Clonard. Kieran spent seven years at Aranmore on Galway Bay with St Enda and then went to a monastery in the centre of Ireland called Isel. Forced to leave by the monks because of what they considered his excessive charity, he spent some time on *Inis Aingin* (Hare Island, West Cork or Galway Bay) and with eight companions, migrated to a spot on the banks of the Shannon in Offaly, here he founded a monastery in 545 that became the now famous Clonmacnoise, renowned for centuries as the great centre of Irish learning, and was its Abbot. Many extravagant miracles and tales are attributed to him and he is one of the twelve apostles of Ireland.

Lower down the hill from the oratory is the Saint's well

KILBRICKAN

(N53°21 W009°37)

On the south Connemara peninsula near Rosmuc is the village of Kilbrickan *(Cill Bhriocáin)* and on a height, together with the local graveyard, stands this attractive little late medieval chapel (L4.9m x W3.2m) dedicated to St Briocain. It apparently stands on the site of an earlier chapel and is now the subject of a research project by the students of the local school.

Remains of St Briocain's late medieval chapel

There is a doorway with a roughly dressed segmented arch in the south wall and a flat-headed window in the east gable. There are aumbries in the east and west gables. This graveyard also contains a holy well and the rectangular foundations of a second building (L12.8m x W4.8m) which might have been a priest's house.

This saint may have been the St Briccéne who was the Abbot of the Toomregan *(Túaim Drecon)* Monastery in Co Cavan, who was reputed to be also a famous surgeon. But more likely, as with Ciaran, he would have been related to Brecán of Aran.

St Briocain's Well

above: Remains of St Briocain's late medieval chapel   below: Adjoining graveyard at east gable

CORUCONA ISLAND

(N53°14 W009°41)

Five miles south south west of Lettermore Bridge (one mile south east of Lettermullen Bridge) on *Oileán Garomna*, and in the townland of *An Máimín*, stand the ruins of an early medieval abbey featuring both the abbey and remains of the monks living quarters at the west end. The abbey now stands in a well occupied graveyard and has been the subject of a FAS youth project undertaken in 1980's to preserve this remaining structure.

Maumeen Abbey

Access to the abbey is via a laneway off the main road just north of Lettermullen Bridge. Alternatively there is a small ancient pathway along the southern shore of the island which also serves a small harbour which may also have been used by the monks to the south side of the abbey.

Situated in a sheltered location to the south of Ballynakill Lough this is a now well preserved early medieval ruin (L10.15m x W5.5m). The doorway, with chamfered jambs and lintel, is set off-centre in the west wall and there is a tall round-headed window in the east wall. The surrounding graveyard contains mainly modern burials. It is not apparent to whom the abbey was dedicated, nor which order it housed.

opposite: Altar and east gable   above: North aspect   below: West wall

TRAWBAUN
Church

(N53°14 W009°39)

On the east shore of *Oileán Garomna*, four and a half miles south of Lettermore Bridge and at the entrance to Greatman's Bay stands the little late medieval chapel (L5.3m x W4m) at *An Trá Bhán* in the townland of *Tír an Fhia*. This is undoubtedly one of the most beautifully kept ancient chapels in the area and is referred to by Roderic O'Flaherty as the Pilgrim's

The Pilgrim's Church

Church. There is a chamfered, pointed-arch doorway in the south west wall and a plain window in the south east gable with an altar below. Beam-holes in the north west and south east gables suggest the former presence of a loft. There are also many graves now situated in the little

enclosure, although some are also inside the little chapel itself and sadly one of these has been made room for by cutting out part of the altar.

In the tradition of these ancient Christian settlements it is situated directly by the sea. The picture on the next page shows just how neatly and close to the sea such settlements were, just above the high-tide lines.

opposite: Altar at east gable   above: South door   below: An Tra Bhan chapel at low tide

BARRADERRY Church

(N53°14 W009°34)

One and a half miles south east of the village of Carraroe and on the edge of Cashla Bay stand the ruins of the medieval Church of *Barr an Doire*. It can be reached on the far side of the present graveyard and the easiest pathway is along the rocky seashore which just allows one to pass at high tide. This is part of one of the largest parishes in the area stretching from

Barr an Doire Church

this coastline inland as far as Lough Corrib to the north. Sadly the church is not kept in the best condition with a widespread growth of ivy on the gable walls and a great deal of rubble and briars inside. There is a mounted gravestone outside in memory of Revd Dommo P O'Roarke, 1818.

Cashla Bay is a busy thoroughfare in these modern times with constant traffic in and out of Rossaveel Harbour, on the opposite shore, which serves as the principal harbour for the fishing fleets of the west coast as well as for the ferry service to the neighbouring Aran Islands.

The west gable features an interesting window design of curvilinear tracery, showing some intricate 'sunburst' designs on the upper facing, which together with the Gothic door, would indicate dating of the building as late medieval.

East window

East gable   *Blocked north door*

Properly known as *Teampall Inis Adhaimh*, this medieval church (L15.6m x W5m) is, however, attributed locally to St *Mocán* or *Smocán,* who may have come from Aran, but there is really nothing known of him.

There is a robbed doorway in the south wall, the scattered fragments of which indicate that it had a pointed arch and moulded architrave. Directly opposite, on the north wall, is a later doorway with a pointed arch. A cusped ogee-headed window in the east gable has decorated spandels and a hood moulding. There is a later internal division at the west end, perhaps with a gallery above, possibly indicating a priest's quarters.

NB. The name Mocan also refers to a Transylvanian shepherd from the Carparthian Mountains of Romania. Nowadays it also refers to anyone living in those mountains.

BANRAGHBAUN SOUTH

(N53°14 W009°28)

1.5 km (2.5ml) WSW of Inverin at *An Bhánrach Bhán Theas* on the seashore and near the eastern entrance to Cashla Bay is to be found a burial ground *(Reilig Mhaorais)* of relatively modern appearance at the mouth of a small stream. It is reputedly the site of one of the monastic foundations of St Columcille and the site of a former church.

Burial ground

Certainly nothing of great antiquity seems to remain there today and it would have been a very exposed and wild site over the centuries since it faces into the prevailing south westerly winds and weather. It is nevertheless a very picturesque burial ground containing many ancient stones.

below: Altar erected in 1990 outside the graveyard and facing the seashore

St Columcille is particularly known for having founded the celtic monastery on the island of Iona off Scotland where the Book of Kells was created. He lived from 521 to 597 AD, about 60 years after St Patrick. Born in Donegal his name was 'Colum' meaning dove; Columcille meaning Dove of the Church.

St Columcille was one of the strongest advocates of the monastic movement and is said to have been instrumental in starting nearly 100 settlements including those at Derry, Durrow and Kells. He was 44 years old when he left Ireland to found the famous monastery on Iona to which so many now make pilgrimage each year.

There is also a natural boulder situated nearby and to the south west along the seashore which is known as *Mullán Cholmcille*, or St Columcille's Boat. As it can be seen to resemble the prow of a boat (even with sails) it is held in folk lore that Columcille would have sailed on this from Aran!

His Feast Day is celebrated on June 9th.

above: Small stream near which this settlement was founded   below: St Columcille's Stone Boat

The Early Monastic Era

What had begun as a lay movement during the 3rd century in the deserts of Egypt had spread and developed along our west and other coastlines of Ireland and Wales to become one of our most unique items of heritage. This early monastic movement in Ireland mostly existed amongst close autonomous communities and so their settlements formed an integral part of what became local religious families based on the confines of what was known as a *tuath* or *lios*. But, away from these remote island settlements off the west coast such monastic communities further inland would have had a greater population surrounding them and obviously would have been more highly developed. Their lands may have been gifts from the local aristocrats of society and many of the monks may well have been born into these monastic communities or were working for or of the social elite. Such communities would have occupied the more fertile inland areas. The only ones who can be said to have deliberately chosen a particular style of life were the ascetics and there must have been something in the Gaelic spirit that was deeply moved by the more ascetic nature of this early monasticism, and naturally drawn to it, hence the existence of the unique sites that are the subject of this guide.

In contrast to the lives of the more populous inland communities there seems to be little that has been recorded of the daily life of the island monk. There is no doubt that these island and coastal settlements were bleak, stormy and isolated for the greater part of the year and that the monks would have suffered much cold and damp in these bare stone isolated dwellings. Yet they obviously had tremendous skills as stonemasons, metalworkers, farmers, mariners and artists, which together with their writing of manuscripts, copying of the gospels, religious and daily disciplines is a testimony to their hardiness, skills and ability to survive over the centuries. Stone was obviously in plentiful supply for their buildings and the sea provided much in the way of food although the surveys conducted on High Island show a remarkable ability in farming and even the construction of a horizontal mill to grind their corn. But apart from the sheer physical nature of their hard and remote life they would also have had their ecclesiastical disciplines and times of meditation around which their lives existed.

The daily services of the church were collectively called the 'hours' or *opus dei,* and fixed at certain times during the day. According to Hughes & Hamlin in their book, *Celtic Monasticism,* these hours would differ in winter or summer. "It will be least confusing if we imagine the monastic day at the summer or winter equinox (20th March or 23rd September), when the day and the night are of equal length. The monks went to bed when the sun went down, slept and then rose for nocturnes, the night office, round about the middle of the night. At dawn they attended lauds. The three daytime hours are terce, sext (midday) and none, which are the third, sixth and ninth hours, and on the sundials found on some sites these hours are marked. Vespers was said in the evening. This gives six 'hours'. Occasionally tracts refer to compline and prime, which would be the prayers said on going to bed and rising". Mass would then be celebrated on Sundays and feast-days.

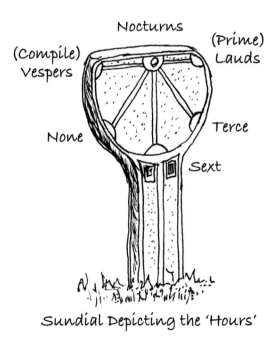

Sundial Depicting the 'Hours'

In some cases these remote settlements were not the first to occupy these sites. Archaeological research has shown that they were often built on earlier bronze age remains, this was the case on both High and Omey Islands. These early Christians would likely have also encountered many difficulties in their work as they sought to introduce their beliefs amongst the local clans who would have been steeped in their own dramatic religious cults. Yet this Christianity seemed to have been well absorbed by the Gaelic society and adapted to its own needs. Little would appear to have changed in this society until the coming of the Vikings. Their occupation of lonely island sites may have been both natural positions on the watery highways as well as being strategic places a pace away from these clans and communities a little further inland.

Whilst little detail appears to be known of the life of the Irish ascetics, many magical tales did surround these early saints and belief in magic was obviously strong amongst the local clans. Conversions may therefore have taken quite some time to effect since the old ideas and customs would have been very much part of everyday life in such matters as fertility, birth and death, the growing of food, the presence of wild animals and places of sacred ritual. The clan chiefs too were very much part of the ancient druidical system so their permission to spread this new faith was essential for these early Christian monks. As ascetics they may well have been inclined to various degrees of self denial, but they were also very aware and appreciative of the wild life and nature that surrounded them as evidenced by such references (from the Annals) in their many writings.

Many of these early saints were then to follow that earlier injunction that encouraged the North African ascetics to ultimately leave family and clan so we find them and their followers venturing back into the wilds of Europe where they were to provide classical education and ultimately to found such well-known monasteries such as at Louvain, Basel & Bobbio.

⩕⩕⩕ Monasteries founded by St Columban	⋔ Church	✝ Centre of Learning
	⩕ Monastery	໑ Irish Bishop Abroad
✝ Important early Irish monastic site	⋔ Hospice	⋒ Later Irish Monastery
ໄ Route followed by St Columban	⊕ Hermit	

Meanwhile, their own early settlements in Connemara were to suffer their first destructions around the year 800 when the Vikings began to raid the islands and monasteries, which would have yielded much in the way of ecclesiastical treasure and art. This continued until just after 1000 and the history of the area remained a turbulent one. The O'Flaherty clan were driven into Connemara by the Normans and O'Connors and ruled there between 1200 and 1600, during which time they too were instrumental in founding many of the later medieval churches. Further inland the monastic movement practically ended with the coming of the Vikings and over 100 monasteries closed across the country and those that survived became more secularised. The Irish church was then without the protection of the monastic system and sought help from the secular powers. This was ultimately to lead to a complete change from a semi-independent and local monastic church life to the introduction of the diocesan system which we have today.

There is a reference in the chronicle of Prosper of Aquitane to the sending of Palladius by Pope Celestine 1 (422-31) to be 'first bishop to the Irish believing in Christ'. Whilst there is no certain connection between Palladius and Patrick, it is generally agreed that Patrick's mission to Ireland was not later than 431. So, although he was sent to those few Christians who were already in Ireland he is certainly credited with the major work and spread of the faith throughout the land, but it is likely that he was not long preceded by these remarkable ascetics who had arrived on our coasts via the ocean highway. Theirs was a truly monastic era and no part of any diocesan system which was not initiated until the Synod of Rathbreasail in 1111.

These early Christian sites are part of the highly significant landmarks in the rich kaleidoscope of Connemara's past history and the remarkable people who brought such culture and art to its shores. It is hoped that these monuments may yet be preserved, valued and recognised for future generations.

BIBLIOGRAPHY / FURTHER READING

Chadwick, Nora K, *Age of the Saints in the Early Celtic Church*, Oxford University Press 1961

Clifden & Connemara Heritage Group, *Connemara*, Connacht Tribune 1995 ISBN 0791 94SX

Comerford, Richard Vincent, *Inventing the Nation - Ireland*, Hodder Arnold 2003

Fleming, John, *Gille of Limerick*, Four Courts Press 2001 ISBN 1-85182-477-4

Gibbons, Michael & Hogan, Dave, *Inis Bó Finne, A Guide to the Natural History and Archaeology*, Connemara Field Studies Centre 1992

Hotz SJ, Dr. Robert, *The Origins of Christian Monasticism (The Anchorites in the Egyptian Desert)* Swissair Gazette, Verlag A Vetter, Zurich, December 1985

Hughes, Kathleen & Hamlin, Ann, *Celtic Monasticism*, Seabury Press 1981 ISBN 08164-2302-4

Killanin, Lord & Duignan, Michael V, *The Shell Guide to Ireland*, Ebury Press 1967

Kilroy, Patricia, *The Story of Connemara*, Gill & McMillan 1989 ISBN 0-7171-1660-3

MacGearailt, Gearoid, *Celts & Normans*, Gill & McMillan 1969

Office of Public Works, *Archaeological Inventory of Co. Galway, Vol 1*, West Galway, 1993

O'Flaherty, Roderic, Notes by Hardiman, James, *H-Iar Connaught, 1684*, 1846

Quinn, Bob, *Atlantean*, Quartet Books, London 1986 ISBN 0-7043-2524-1

Robinson, Tim, *Connemara (Part 1:Introduction and Gazetteer)*, Folding Landscapes 1990

Ryan, John, *Irish Monasticism, Origins and Early Development*, first published 1931

Toulson, Shirley, *The Celtic Alternative*, Rider Press 1990 ISBN 0-7126-1478-8

White Marshall, Jenny & Rourke, Grellan D, *High Island*, Town House & Country House 2000 ISBN 186059-121-3

INDEX